Narcissist Unmasked

Narcissistic Wifes, Volume 5

Dr Paul J Peloquin Sr, PhD

Published by Dr Paul J Peloquin Sr, PhD, 2025.

NARCISSIST UNMASKED

First edition. June 20, 2025.

ISBN: 979-8232284145

Written by Dr Paul J Peloquin Sr, PhD.

Narcissist Unmasked:

A Practical Handbook for Identifying and Escaping Female Narcissists

By Dr. Paul J. Peloquin, Sr., PhD

Preface

This handbook is written for men who have found themselves entangled in emotionally abusive relationships with narcissistic women. As someone who has walked this road, I, Dr. Paul J. Peloquin, Sr., PhD, offer not just insight—but survival strategies. You are not alone. The pain, confusion, and isolation you feel is real. This guide is designed to validate your experience and equip you with clear steps to identify, escape, and heal from the control and chaos of a narcissistic partner.

Chapter 1: Recognize the Mask

Narcissistic women rarely show their true face at the beginning of a relationship. Instead, they present a carefully crafted mask of charm, attentiveness, and idealized affection. To the outside world, she might be admired—respected, even envied. But behind closed doors, she begins to show control, emotional cruelty, and calculated manipulation. Dr. Paul J. Peloquin, Sr., PhD emphasizes that recognizing the mask is the first critical step to reclaiming your life. Many men struggle to reconcile the woman they fell in love with and the person she becomes once control is established. The 'ideal partner' image was a performance—an audition designed to hook your emotional investment. Signs of the mask include sudden mood swings, coldness in private, belittling your efforts, or twisting your words. She may praise you in public and degrade you in private. This duplicity is intentional. The mask shields her from accountability and manipulates your perception. Accepting that the mask was never real can be painful—but it's also liberating. It marks the beginning of clear vision and opens the door to authentic healing. You are not imagining the abuse. You are seeing the truth behind the illusion.

Chapter 2: Understand the Manipulation

Manipulation is the lifeblood of the narcissistic relationship. It is how she gains control, maintains dominance, and erodes your sense of self — all while appearing blameless to the outside world. You may not realize it at first, but over time, you find yourself questioning your memory, your emotions, your worth, and eventually, your sanity.

As I know firsthand how subtle and systemic this manipulation can be. You do not walk into a narcissist's trap — you get walked into it. Slowly. Step by step. With compliments, seduction, sympathy, and charm. Then, just when you are emotionally invested and disoriented, the rules change.

THE ILLUSION OF LOVE

Narcissistic manipulation often starts with excessive flattery and attention — the infamous "love bombing" phase. She makes you feel like the only man in the world. Your values, your dreams, your pain — all seem to matter to her. She may even say things like, "I've never felt this way about anyone," or, "You understand me like no one ever has."

This isn't love. It's data collection.

She's learning your vulnerabilities, your hopes, your triggers. All of it will later be weaponized — not to uplift you, but to control you.

Gaslighting: The Destruction of Reality

One of the most insidious manipulation tactics used by narcissistic women is gaslighting. You bring up a concern, and she flips it. You recall an event, and she denies it. You express pain, and she mocks it or accuses you of being too sensitive. Or she has same pain.

Example:

> You: "You were really cold last night in front of my friends."
>
> Her: "You're imagining things. You always twist what I say. Maybe you're the one with the problem."

Before long, you start wondering if you are the problem. You apologize for things you didn't do. You begin doubting your own memory. You feel like you're walking through fog — and the only light source is her opinion.

Triangulation: Divide and Control

She introduces comparisons and external influences to destabilize you. This may be an "ex" she still talks to, a male friend she flirts with, or a female friend she confides in about your shortcomings.

She may say things like:

- "My ex never got this upset when I went out."
- "Maybe you should be more like Dan — he listens."
- "I told Rachel what you said, and even she thinks you're overreacting."

This triangulation tactic isolates you emotionally. You stop talking to friends because she's already poisoned the well. You stop voicing your concerns because you fear she'll twist it to someone else. You begin shrinking.

Blame Shifting and Projection

Nothing is ever her fault. If she's angry, it's because you "made" her angry. If she lies, it's because you "forced her to." If she cheats, it's because you weren't attentive enough.

She will:

- Project her behavior onto you ("Are you hiding something from me?" — when she's the one being deceptive)
- Shift the topic when confronted ("Let's talk about how you're always so negative.")
- Use your empathy as a weapon ("If you really loved me, you'd understand.")

The goal is always the same: to stay in control and avoid responsibility.

The Emotional Yo-Yo

A narcissistic woman keeps you on a cycle of emotional highs and lows — affection, followed by punishment; validation, followed by rejection. You never know where you stand. This unpredictability creates dependency.

It's like a gambler at a slot machine. You know that occasionally, you'll get a little reward — a kind word, a hug, a flash of the woman you fell for. So you stay. You hope. You beg. But the longer you stay, the more you lose.

RECLAIMING YOUR MIND: How to Break the Cycle

Understanding manipulation is about clarity. Once you name what's happening, the fog begins to lift.

Checklist for Identifying Emotional Manipulation:

- Do you feel guilty for expressing your needs?
- Do you often second-guess your memory of conversations?
- Does she deny or twist your words frequently?
- Do you feel you can never "get it right" no matter how hard you try?
- Have you stopped talking to friends or family out of embarrassment?

If you answered yes to most of these — you are being manipulated. And it's not your fault.

Tools to Begin Taking Back Control

1. Start documenting — conversations, behaviors, gaslighting examples. This validates your experience.
2. Name the tactic — every time she manipulates you, say to yourself: "That's gaslighting. That's projection."

3. Refuse to argue on her terms — if she shifts blame or twists logic, end the conversation.
4. Rebuild outside support — talk to a therapist, a trusted friend, or a men's support group.
5. Affirm your own reality — trust what you see and feel. That's not weakness — that's survival.

A Word from Dr. Paul J. Peloquin, Sr., PhD

I stayed far too long in a relationship where my mind was constantly being bent, questioned, and rewritten. What kept me there was hope. And the feeling of "feeling bad for her" What saved me was God.

Manipulation only works when you don't see it for what it is. But once you do — you begin to gain power she can no longer take.

Stay grounded. Stay aware. The next steps in this guide will walk you further down the path to freedom.

Chapter 3: The Mask of Empathy — When Caring is Calculated

Empathy is the cornerstone of human connection. It's what allows us to feel seen, heard, and safe in the presence of another. For most people, empathy is genuine—a natural response to another's joy or suffering. But for the female narcissist, empathy is not felt; it is performed. This chapter explores how narcissists weaponize pseudo-empathy to manipulate, disarm, and ultimately control their partners.

As I, have seen through both research and lived experience, the female narcissist's version of empathy is nothing more than a calculated strategy. She learns the language of compassion without ever feeling its spirit. This deceptive mimicry can leave even the most emotionally intelligent man questioning their own judgment.

THE EMPATHY FACADE

She seems deeply caring. She remembers your birthday, supports your career, listens intently when you speak. But take a closer look—her empathy has strings attached. Her support turns cold if your success threatens her spotlight, or if your plan doesn't come to pass. Her listening ear closes when your pain doesn't serve her image as the "loving partner."

Many male survivors recall the early stages of the relationship as "perfect." She was attentive, nurturing, and emotionally tuned in. That wasn't empathy; that was mirroring—a technique narcissists use to reflect back what their target most wants to see. Once the bond is formed, that mask begins to crack.

Empathy as a Manipulation Tool

Genuine empathy leads to action based on care and concern. The female narcissist uses a counterfeit version to manipulate behavior:

- Feigning concern when she is being scrutinized by others: "I only said that because I care so deeply."
- Offering comfort just long enough to regain control: "I know I hurt you, but I was just overwhelmed. You know how emotional I can be."
- Using selective empathy to support superiority: "I understand why other women would feel that way, but I'm more evolved than that."

This is not empathy—it's emotional theater. Every tear, hug, or soft tone is delivered with purpose, not feeling.

The Empathy Withdrawal Tactic

Another hallmark of the narcissistic woman is the removal of empathy as punishment. This withdrawal is sudden, chilling, and effective:

- You open up about stress, and she responds with indifference or disdain.
- You express needs, and she accuses you of being needy or weak.
- You become vulnerable, and she turns that vulnerability into a weapon during your next argument.

This tactic destabilizes your emotional foundation. Over time, you may learn to suppress your emotions altogether believing you are the problem, not realizing that her conditional empathy was designed to mold your behavior through fear and confusion chaos.

Empathic Echo vs. Emotional Depth

In working with males, with similar characteristics. I have developed a tool I call the "Empathic Echo Test." Ask yourself:

> "Does she show consistent emotional depth, or does she simply echo what I express?"

A narcissistic woman will mimic concern but rarely follows through. She may say, "That must be hard for you," but never checks in later. She offers words without weight. This lack of follow-through is a critical red flag—genuine empathy leaves a trace. Hers leaves doubt.

Why Men Struggle to See Through the Mask

Many men, especially those raised to believe in second chances and the power of love, are more susceptible to the illusion of female empathy. We want to believe she means well. We rationalize: She is just stressed. She had a distressing day. I'm overreacting?

As I learned firsthand, this internal narrative becomes a trap. You defend her actions to others. You make excuses. You bend further to prove your worth hoping to trigger the same warmth you once saw in her eyes. But that warmth was never real. It was bait.

FROM EMPATHY TO EMPTINESS

The emotional contrast becomes striking over time. The woman who once cried when you shared childhood trauma now dismisses your pain. She once praised your sensitivity but now calls you "too emotional" or "unstable." This swing isn't confusion—it's control. I have emails she sent to her friends when we first met, "I was a God to her then".

Understanding this shift is crucial. Her empathy was a tool to hook you. Her coldness is a tool to control you.

DR. PAUL'S PRACTICAL Tools: Spotting Fake Empathy

Use these questions to evaluate whether you are dealing with authentic compassion or narcissistic mimicry:

1. Does her empathy extend to others, or only appear when it benefits her?
2. Are her words supported by action?
3. Does she respond differently when no one is watching?
4. Are your emotions used against you later?
5. Do you feel emotionally safe or emotionally managed?

If you answered "no" to most and "yes" to the last, you may be in a relationship with a female narcissist.

Final Thoughts: The Cost of Pseudo-Empathy

A woman who cannot truly feel for you cannot truly love you.

What she offers is not partnership, but performance. And the longer you stay hoping for real empathy, the more of yourself you lose.

Empathy is not a luxury—it is a requirement for healthy love. And if she cannot give it, no amount of patience, explanation, or effort will change that.

Chapter 4: Isolation by Design — Cutting You Off to Control You

One of the most subtle and sinister tactics used by a female narcissist is isolation. Not all at once, and rarely by force. Instead, it happens slowly—strategically. At first, it feels like deep intimacy: she wants all your time, all your energy, all your love. But gradually, closeness morphs into containment.

In this chapter, I, will walk you through how female narcissists isolate their partners—not with chains, but with charm and control. If you have ever found yourself wondering why you feel so alone while in a relationship, this chapter may provide the clarity you need.

The Illusion of "Us Against the World"

At the start, the narcissist builds a powerful emotional bubble. She tells you, "We don't need anyone else," or "No one understands us like we do." It feels romantic—even empowering. But this is the first move in a long game designed to disconnect you from your external sources of truth, support, and self-worth.

You begin canceling plans with friends. You stop calling family as often. You share less about the relationship with people you trust. And soon, your world shrinks until she is the center of it.

What you may not realize is this: isolation is not a symptom of love—it is a strategy of domination.

Why Narcissists Fear Your Independence

To the female narcissist, your independence is a threat. Your friends remind you of who you were before her. Your family might question her behavior. Your hobbies and passions take attention away from her. So she sets out to cut those ties, one by one.

- She criticizes your friends: "I don't think they really support you."
- She sows doubt about your family: "I can't believe you don't go see your mom more ,some son you are."
- She monopolizes your time: "Why would you want to go without me?"
- She subtly undermines your passions: "You spend more time with your computer than with me."

Her goal? To become your only mirror, the sole voice in your emotional world. And once she succeeds, your identity begins to dissolve.

Emotional Isolation: The Invisible Cage

Not all isolation is physical. In fact, the most dangerous kind is emotional. Even when you're surrounded by others, you feel unseen. You don't speak freely. You censor yourself. You avoid sharing your relationship struggles because you fear being shamed, dismissed—or worse, disbelieved.

This is how emotional isolation works:

- You no longer feel safe expressing needs; she waits for right time to record you without you knowing.
- You start questioning your own thoughts and feelings.
- You feel guilty for wanting time away from her.
- You fear judgment if you tell anyone what's really happening.

You may even start defending her actions, because she has trained you to think you are the one with the problem.

Dr. Paul's Warning Signs of Narcissistic Isolation

In my clinical work and personal journey, I have identified key signs that a narcissistic partner is isolating a man. Ask yourself:

- ❖ Has she made you feel guilty for spending time with others?
- ❖ Do you feel you can no longer confide in old friends or family?
- ❖ Has she reframed your friends as enemies?
- ❖ Are you second-guessing your beliefs of her behavior?
- ❖ Do you feel emotionally starved—even when she is right next to you?

If you find yourself nodding "yes" to these questions, you may be experiencing narcissistic isolation. Recognizing this is the first step to reclaiming your autonomy.

The worst part of it all, was even though I was not truly happy, and lost without her, till I was able to look from the outside looking in. And experience life without that around me. It's been almost 2 years since Ive even seen her in court room through Zoom and she discussed me to hear her or even seen her.

The Trap of "You're All I Have"

Another manipulative technique the female narcissist uses is playing the victim. She will say things like:

- "Everyone always abandons me—don't you leave me too."
- "You're the only one who understands me." I love you.
- "I have no one else but you."
- I Love you with all my heart! Then-cut you down.

This may trigger your empathy and sense of duty. But remember—this is not true vulnerability. It is emotional blackmail. It is designed to make you feel responsible for her emotional well-being, which gives her more control over your decisions, time, and freedom.

Why Isolation Works So Well

Isolation works because it does not look like abuse. It looks like love, like intensity, like devotion. But healthy relationships do not require you to lose your tribe, your voice, or your identity.

The female narcissist understands that if you stay connected to those who love you, you may eventually leave her. So, she ensures you feel trapped, emotionally, and logistically.

You might ask yourself:

- Where would I go?
- Who would believe me?
- How would I even start over?
- Im goin to be alone at my age?

If you are thinking those thoughts, know this: she planted them.

Reversing the Isolation: Rebuilding Your World

Escaping isolation requires deliberate effort—but it is absolutely possible. Here is where to begin:

1. **Reconnect Slowly** – Reach out to one friend or family member you trust. Just one. You do not have to explain everything right away. Just reopen the door.
2. **Use Neutral Language** – Narcissists often smear their victims. To avoid escalating conflict while planning your exit, use neutral language with mutual contacts.
3. **Find Objective Support** – Whether it is a counselor, coach, support group, or spiritual guide, connect with someone outside her circle who can offer clear feedback.
4. **Reclaim Your Passions** – Start small. Go for a walk, journal, play music, or revisit a hobby. These acts reconnect you with you.
5. **Create a Safety Net** – Begin quietly creating emotional and logistical supports. Prepare finances, plan housing, and document behavior if needed.
6. **Me**, I authored books about her and my life with that!

Dr. Paul's Final Insight: Isolation Is a Choice She Makes—But Freedom Is a Choice You Can Make

Isolation does not happen by accident. It is engineered. And no matter how entangled you feel, you are not alone. You are not weak. You are not crazy.

The narcissist may control your environment, but she cannot control your mind unless you give her that power.

You have the right to exist as a whole person—independent, connected, and free.

Chapter 5: Shame Games — How Guilt Keeps You Trapped

Shame is one of the most powerful tools in the narcissist's arsenal. And when wielded by a skilled female narcissist, it does not come in the form of open hostility—it comes subtly, wrapped in concern, or delivered with a sigh and a disappointed look. It says: You failed me. You should be better. You are the problem. And then "I LOVE YOU."

I have seen this psychological manipulation in my personal life. Many men fall into the trap of believing that if they can just do more, be more, or fix themselves, their partner will finally be happy. But this is a LIE. The female narcissist is not looking for healing—she is feeding on your guilt.

The Cycle of Control: From Idealization to Condemnation

At first, she lifts you up—praises your character, your accomplishments, your potential. You feel like the best version of yourself in her presence. But once you are emotionally invested, the tide turns. I wanted to stay in the complex I was in; we would get a larger one, NO, she wanted me to move in with her it would be cheaper. And away from my family.

She begins to chip away at your confidence with offhand remarks, comparisons, or reminders of how you're not meeting her ever-shifting standards:

- "I thought you were different than other men."
- "Why can't you be more like so-and-so?"

- "You never listen to me."
- "If you really loved me, you'd try harder."

These are not just complaints. They are carefully constructed shame triggers designed to keep you in a permanent state of apology and submission.

Understanding the Difference Between Guilt and Shame

Guilt says, I did something wrong.

Shame says, there is something wrong with me.

Female narcissists blur these lines on purpose. They do not just criticize your actions—they attack your character. Over time, you may start internalizing their judgments:

- Maybe I am selfish.
- Maybe I am too sensitive.
- Maybe I am the reason we keep fighting.
- Nothing I do make her genuinely happy/Why?

As a result, you stop asserting your needs. You shrink. You try harder to earn her approval—never realizing that the game is rigged.

Common Shame Tactics Used by Female Narcissists

1. **Silent Treatment as Punishment**

She withdraws affection and communication, leaving you anxious and desperate to fix what you "did wrong."

1. **Public Humiliation Disguised as Jokes**

She mocks or criticizes you in front of others, then gaslights you: "It was just a joke—don't be so sensitive."

1. **Comparisons to Exes or Other Men**

She uses past partners or male friends as measuring sticks, implying you will never measure up. Or the ones she is communicating with in face book, instagram, TikTok etc.

1. **Emotional Withholding**

She withholds love, intimacy, or support until you grovel or apologize—often for things you did not do.

1. **Rewriting History**

She reframes past events to cast herself as the victim and you as the aggressor, making you feel ashamed for standing up for yourself.

Each of these tactics is designed to destabilize your emotional core—and they work.

Why Men Fall for Shame-Based Control

Many men are raised with an internal script that rewards sacrifice, stoicism, and loyalty. Narcissistic women exploit these values. They frame your natural instincts—to care, protect, and fix—as signs of weakness or obligation.

"You're the man—you should be able to handle this."

"You made vows, didn't you?"

"If you leave, you're abandoning me."

Statements like these are not appeals to love—they are traps. They make you believe that standing up for yourself is selfish, and that self-respect is betrayal.

Dr. Paul's Reflections: My Personal Battle with Shame

There was a time in my own relationship where I found myself constantly apologizing. Not just for mistakes, but for existing. If I voiced my feelings, I was "too emotional." If I stayed silent, I was "cold and distant." No matter what I did, it was not enough or right. Would be flipped.

I began to believe her version of me was the truth.

The turning point came when I realized: shame was not my conscience—it was her control. Once I separated the voice of the narcissist from the voice of truth, I began reclaiming my power. And so can you. No, it is not easy in fact it took years for me to really get it! Through many separations and break ups for months at a time till this last time over just words said by both of us. On December 18th, 2023. The day it ended. And then the pain started.

The Cost of Living Under Guilt

Shame does not just hurt emotionally—it rewires your self-concept. It causes:

- Chronic self-doubt
- Anxiety and depression
- Decision paralysis
- Fear of conflict
- Emotional numbness
- Reluctance to trust again
- Creativity is gone...

In long-term relationships, this toxic shame creates an identity crisis. You forget who you were before her. You begin defining your worth by her moods.

But here's the truth: you are not responsible for her happiness, her emotions, or her approval.

Breaking the Cycle: Tools for Shame Recovery

1. Name It to Reclaim It

When you feel guilt, pause and ask: "Is this true guilt, or shame manipulation?" If it's shame, identify the source.

1. Track the Patterns

Journal interactions that left you feeling "less than." Over time, you'll see that the shame wasn't random—it was routine.

1. Replace Her Voice with Yours

Create affirmations that counteract her narratives. Example:

Her voice: "You're too emotional."
Your truth: "My emotions are valid and healthy."

1. **Talk to an Outside Ally**

Whether a therapist, friend, or coach—choose someone not influenced by her. Let them reflect the truth back to you.

1. **Rebuild Your Moral Compass**

You are not bad. You are not broken. You've been lied to. Begin defining your own sense of right and wrong—apart from her opinions.

Dr. Paul's Truth: You Were Never the Monster She Made You Believe You Were

If you take one thing from this chapter, let it be this:

Guilt can be resolved. Shame can be released. You can come home to yourself.

The narcissist used your compassion as a weapon—but that same compassion, when turned inward, becomes your greatest source of healing.

Chapter 6: Gaslighted and Gut-Checked — When You No Longer Trust Your Own Mind

There is a moment in every narcissistically abusive relationship when the victim stops trusting what they see, hear, and feel. Reality becomes negotiable. Memory becomes questionable. And the gut instinct (as they will use as a tool to make you think they should have listened to their friends about you)—the very core of human self-protection—becomes muted, overridden by confusion and self-doubt.

This moment is no accident. It is the result of a calculated psychological tactic known as gaslighting.

What is Gaslighting?

Gaslighting is a form of psychological abuse in which the narcissist systematically distorts reality, denies facts, and undermines your belief until you question your sanity.

It starts small:

- "You're remembering it wrong."
- "That's not what I said."
- "You are too sensitive.
- All you see is what YOU see.

And escalates into full-blown reality reversal:

- "You're making things up."

- "That never happened."
- "You're crazy."

Over time, you begin to second-guess your own memory, even when you know the truth.

How Gaslighting Works in Stages

The female narcissist doesn't just lie—she restructures truth to serve her image and maintain dominance. Here's how it unfolds:

1. **Subtle Denial**

You mention something she said last week. She insists it never happened. It's not aggressive—just dismissive.

1. **Emotional Redirection**

You express hurt or confusion. She turns the tables: "Why are you always attacking me?" Suddenly, you are the aggressor.

1. **Undermining Confidence**

She brings up your "bad memory," your "paranoia," your "overthinking." You start wondering if she is right.

1. **Rewriting the Narrative**

Past events are retold with her as the victim and you as the villain. The more she tells it, the more you start to believe it. As week as her depth of her narrative.

1. **Full Mental Reprogramming**

You stop trusting yourself. You rely on her for "what really happened." You live in a state of chronic self-doubt.

This is not miscommunication. It is strategic erasure of your reality.

All these books Ive written are from years of notes and recording of me venting my experiences and thoughts. And from that Ive been able to formulate the books and advise I have.

THE INTERNAL COLLAPSE: When Your Gut Goes Quiet

One of the most damaging effects of gaslighting is the silencing of your intuition. That feeling in your gut that says "this isn't right" becomes muffled beneath layers of second-guessing:

- Maybe I'm being too sensitive.
- Maybe I did exaggerate.
- Maybe it really was my fault.

The female narcissist cultivates this doubt not with outright control, but with emotional corrosion. Each denial chips away at your inner compass, until you're not even sure which way is up.

Dr. Paul's Lived Experience: The Moment I Stopped Trusting Myself

I remember standing in the kitchen, arguing over something I knew had happened—a cruel comment she made in front of a friend. But she stared at me, calm, cold, and certain, and said, "That never happened. You must be remembering someone else."

I laughed nervously. I knew I was not wrong. But I still walked away unsure. That's when I realized—I wasn't just dealing with denial. I was dealing with intentional distortion. And that realization was the beginning of my awakening. Never will win any argument ever.

Key Phrases That Signal Gaslighting

Here are common gaslighting lines narcissistic women use to dismantle your reality:

- "You're imagining things."
- "You always twist my words."
- "You're just being dramatic."
- "Stop overreacting."
- "If anyone's abusive, it's you."

The goal isn't just to win the argument—it's to win control over your perception. If she can dominate your reality, she never has to take responsibility for anything.

Why It's So Effective

Gaslighting works because it exploits your:

- Desire for harmony — You want peace, not conflict.
- Sense of fairness — You consider that maybe you did misunderstand.
- Emotional intelligence — Your empathy leads you to question your role.

Ironically, the more self-aware and conscientious you are, the more susceptible you may be. Your strengths become vulnerabilities in her hands.

How to Fight Back Against Gaslighting

Reclaiming your mind starts with trusting your gut again. Here is how:

1. **Start Documenting Everything**

Keep a private log of conversations, dates, and incidents. When your memory is questioned, you'll have the truth in writing.

1. **Set Reality Anchors**

Talk to trusted friends or counselors. Say, "Can I run something by you? Am I overreacting?" Reality-checking with safe people helps reset your perception.

1. **Use Direct Language**

Call it what it is. "You're changing the subject." "That's not what I said." "I'm allowed to feel hurt."

1. **Create Space**

Emotional clarity increases with distance. Even short breaks from the gaslighter—physical or emotional—can restore inner truth.

1. **Rebuild Self-Trust Intentionally**

Make small, independent decisions each day. Prove to yourself that your judgment is still sharp—because it is.

DR. PAUL'S REALITY Reminder: If You Feel Crazy, You're Probably Being Gaslighted

Healthy relationships don't leave you confused and questioning your sanity.

They don't force you to record conversations just to prove your innocence.

They don't make you walk away from arguments wondering if you're losing your mind.

You are not unstable. You are being destabilized.

The good news? Your mind is recoverable. Your gut still works. Your clarity is not gone—it's just been buried beneath her lies.

Chapter 7: The Triangle Trap — How She Uses Others to Divide, Distract, and Dominate

When we think of narcissistic abuse, we often picture one-on-one manipulation. But a skilled female narcissist knows how to expand the playing field. She doesn't just gaslight or shame you—she triangulates. That means she pulls a third person (or multiple people) into the relationship dynamic, not to help, but to control. And discusses our private marriage with them looking for them to agree with her take on the marriage. Then some the real people that are just like her, huh, I've heard her say" she could not stand that person(s) up till now are one of her allies and attach me. And do not even know the truth or why but they just jump in feet first.

WHAT IS TRIANGULATION?

Triangulation is when the narcissist involves a third party to:

- Validate her view of you
- Spark jealousy
- Create competition
- Divide your attention
- Deflect blame
- Preserve control

This third party may be an ex, a friend, a child, a coworker, a therapist—even someone you love and trust. But in the hands of a narcissist, they become pawns in a larger strategy of manipulation.

How She Uses Others to Control You

Here are the most common forms of triangulation a female narcissist may use:

---

1. The Ex-Talk

She brings up an ex-boyfriend—often and favorably. You are constantly compared:

- "He never got so emotional."
- "He used to buy me flowers without being asked."
- "I still talk to him sometimes—he really understands me."

This isn't nostalgia. It's a control tactic. She's planting jealousy and insecurity, making you feel like you're not enough—and that someone else was.

2. The Secret Ally

She creates an alliance with someone who you know and been out to dinners with manytimes, go to beach with us etc. —your friend, sibling, or even your child. She paints herself as misunderstood or victimized, subtly turning others against you:

- "He's just been really moody lately, but I'm trying to be patient."
- "I don't want to say anything bad about him, but I'm really struggling."

She gains their sympathy while undermining your credibility. Now, when you try to explain what's happening, you look like the unstable one.

---

3. The "Expert" Opinion

She quotes her therapist, a book, or even your mutual friend to confirm her behavior and discredit yours:

- "Even my therapist says you're the problem."
- "Everyone agrees you're too controlling."
- "I talked to my mom—she says you're emotionally abusive."

She creates a fake consensus, making you question whether your reality is valid at all.

4. The Child Weaponization

In co-parenting situations, triangulation often involves the child. She paints herself as the loving, stable parent and you as unpredictable, angry, or neglectful. She may say things to your child like:

- "Daddy doesn't love us the same way."
- "He's always upset with me—do you think that's fair?"
- "Let's not tell him about this—it'll just make him mad."
- Or telling you that your children do not want to be around you, (when its truly, they do NOT want to be around HER!

This not only destroys the child's sense of emotional safety—it devastates your parental confidence.

5. THE "NEW GUY" FLIRTATION

She flirts openly (on the internet with social media). With all kinds of men from her past, a coworker, trainer, or male friend— keeping you reacting. If you call it out, she accuses you of being jealous or controlling. But her real motive is to keep you chasing her validation.

Why Triangulation Hurts So Deeply

Triangulation works because it mimics real betrayal—but in a way that keeps her hands clean. She's not technically cheating. She's not directly smearing you. But she's poisoning the well from behind the curtain.

You begin to feel:

- Jealous
- Paranoid
- Isolated
- Unstable
- Desperate for reassurance

And all the while, she watches quietly feeding off the chaos she created.

Dr. Paul's Reflection: I Was in a Relationship with a Crowd

At one point, I realized I was not just dealing with her—I was dealing with her exes, her friends, her family, her therapist. Every disagreement became a court case, and I was always the one on trial. She would record our arguments and send them to her friends. Without me knowing...

She would say, "I talked to my mom, and she agrees you're emotionally distant."

Or "Even your friend said I deserve better."

Or worst of all: "Your own son said he's scared of your anger."

It was psychological warfare—constant, calculated, and camouflaged as "concern."

HOW TO BREAK FREE FROM Triangulation

1. **Recognize It for What It Is**

   When you feel your emotions being manipulated by the mention of others, pause and ask: "Is this triangulation?"

1. **Disengage from the Triangle**

   Don't chase validation. Don't try to "win" the third party. Step out. "I won't compete with your ex. If you miss him, be with him."

1. **Set Boundaries Around Gossip**

"I don't want to hear what your therapist/friend/mother thinks of me unless they tell me directly."

1. Protect Your Relationships

Go directly to the source. If she's speaking for someone close to you, clarify. "Did you really say that about me to her?"

1. **Speak with Authority**

Use phrases like:

- "This is between you and me."
- "Please don't involve others in our private matters."
- "You're creating drama where it doesn't belong."

Dr. Paul's Final Truth: You Are Not the Jealous, Insecure, Toxic Partner She Says You Are

Triangulation makes you feel like you're losing your mind and your relationships. But you're not crazy—you're being played. The narcissist thrives in drama because it keeps you focused on her, not yourself.

You deserve relationships rooted in trust, not manipulation. In honesty, not performance. In clarity, not confusion.

Chapter 8: The Dependence Trap — How She Makes You

Rely on Her to Feel Worthy

It often begins innocently: she makes you feel like the most important man in the world. She praises your strengths, showers you with attention, and tells you how special, different, and irreplaceable you are. For a moment, it feels like you've found heaven.

But what you don't realize—what many don't—is that she's not building you up out of love. She's building dependency.

By the time the mask drops, you're no longer in control of how you feel about yourself. She is.

As, I've witnessed—and lived—the transformation from self-assured man to emotional captive. This chapter explores how female narcissists make you dependent on their validation, then use that dependency to control, diminish, and eventually dismantle you.

The Addiction to Her Approval

At first, it feels like connection. But before long, it becomes addiction. You start measuring your worth based on her reactions:

- If she's happy, you're good.
- If she's withdrawn, you're bad.
- If she's affectionate, you're lovable.
- If she's critical, you're failing.

You begin living for those rare moments of affection and validation—like a gambler pulling the lever, hoping this time the jackpot will hit.

This is not love. This is intermittent reinforcement—a psychological conditioning technique used in gambling and cults. It's intentional.

How She Builds the Trap

The female narcissist creates dependence in three predictable stages:

1. Idealize You

She floods you with admiration:

- "You're unlike anyone I've ever met."
- "You're so intelligent, strong, thoughtful."
- "I feel safe with you."
- I hope you win the Senate race"

You open your heart. You give your trust. You let her in.

2. Withdraw or Criticize

Suddenly, she's colder. More distant. Or begins to nitpick:

- "Why did you say it that way?"
- "You're not trying hard enough."
- "I'm just disappointed."

You scramble to restore the closeness. You think: What did I do wrong? How can I fix this?

3. Reward You (Sporadically)

After days of coldness or silence, she gives you a "good moment":

- A compliment.
- A hug.
- A night of passion.

You feel relief—finally, we are okay again. But what you do not see is that you have just been trained to chase her love like a dog for a treat. It is truly "Pavlov's "Classical conditioning.

Other wise known as "Pavlov's Dog." Conditioned Response "

IVAN PAVLOV (1849-1936):

- A renowned Russian and Soviet physiologist.
- Famous for his work on **classical conditioning**, where a neutral stimulus becomes associated with a meaningful stimulus, eliciting a learned response.
- His most famous experiment involved dogs and the association of a metronome sound with food, leading to salivation even when only the sound was presented.
- Awarded the Nobel Prize in Physiology or Medicine in 1904 for his work on digestion.
- His work significantly influenced the field of psychology and the understanding of learning

Why This Trap Works on Men

As men, we're taught to earn respect, achieve success, and solve problems. When our partner becomes cold or angry, we assume we're doing something wrong—and we try harder.

But in a relationship with a female narcissist, this dynamic gets twisted. No matter how much you give, it's never enough. And the more you try, the more power she gains.

You begin equating your value with her approval.

The Loss of Internal Validation

One of the most damaging aspects of this dynamic is how it hijacks your self-esteem.

You no longer rely on your own sense of accomplishment, your own moral compass, or your own emotional truth. You look to her facial expressions, her tone, her silence. You live in fear of her disapproval—and hunger for her praise.

And slowly, your identity erodes. You don't just want her love—you need it. And that's exactly where she wants you.

Dr. Paul's Experience: I Forgot Who I Was

There was a point where my moods no longer came from within. If she woke up happy, I had a good day. If she was cold, I walked on eggshells. If she gave a compliment, I felt like I mattered again.

One day, I looked in the mirror and couldn't recognize myself. Not physically, but emotionally. I had become a man who couldn't breathe without her approval. That realization was terrifying—but it was also the beginning of my recovery.

Signs You have Fallen into the Dependence Trap

Ask yourself:

✓ Do I feel unworthy when she's angry or disappointed in me?

✓ Do I constantly second-guess my decisions based on how she might react?

✓ Do I find myself doing things I don't agree with just to keep the peace?
✓ Do I feel anxious when I haven't received her approval or affection?
✓ Have I lost confidence in my own judgment and instincts?

If you answered "yes" to most of these, you are not weak—you are conditioned. But you can unlearn it.

How to Reclaim Your Self-Worth

1. **Recognize the Pattern**

Just naming the dynamic helps break its power. Say it clearly: I am being trained to depend on her approval. That's not love—that's control.

1. **Create Internal Anchors**

Write a list of your core values, skills, and strengths. Reconnect with what makes you proud of you—independent of her feedback.

1. **Affirm Your Identity Daily**

Start your morning with truths like:

- "My worth is not defined by her mood."
- "I trust my instincts."
- "I am allowed to feel good without her permission."

1. **Reconnect with Others Who Value You**

Talk with friends, family, mentors—people who knew you before her. Let their words remind you of who you are.

1. **Practice Micro-Acts of Independence**

Make small decisions without her input. Revisit hobbies she dismissed. Spend time alone. These small wins rebuild internal confidence.

Dr. Paul's Truth: Her Validation is Not Oxygen—You Can Breathe Without Her

When you base your self-worth on a narcissist's approval, you are renting your identity from someone who profits by keeping you insecure.

But here's the truth: you are not unlovable, broken, or weak. You are human. And like any human, you have the right to feel good about yourself without conditions.

You do not need her permission to feel whole. That power already belongs to you.

Chapter 9: Drama as a Weapon — When Her Emotions Overshadow Her Accountability

If you've ever found yourself trying to have a calm, reasonable conversation—only to end up managing her tears, her rage, or her panic—then you've experienced one of the most cunning tactics of the female narcissist: weaponized drama.

She turns every confrontation into a performance, every consequence into a catastrophe, and every truth you try to speak into a betrayal. Suddenly, you feel like the villain for even bringing up a legitimate concern.

As I can assure you: this is no accident. It is a deliberate strategy. Narcissistic women use intense emotions—tears, tantrums, threats, and theatrics—not as expressions of genuine feeling, but as tools to deflect blame, gain sympathy, and escape accountability.

THE PURPOSE BEHIND the Performance

Contrary to what you might think, the narcissist's dramatic displays aren't about emotional instability—they're about emotional dominance. When her behavior is questioned or her image is threatened, she has three core objectives:

1. Shift the focus away from her actions
2. Make you feel guilty for hurting her

3. Regain control of the narrative through chaos

If you walk away from an argument confused, exhausted, or apologizing for something she did—you've just been emotionally outmaneuvered.

Types of Narcissistic Drama

Let's break down the most common forms of drama the female narcissist uses to escape responsibility:

1. Crying on Cue

As soon as you bring up an issue—be it a boundary, a broken promise, or emotional neglect—tears begin to flow. Not out of sorrow for hurting you, but sorrow for being "attacked."

You hear:

- "I can't believe you think that about me."
- "You're so cold."
- "I've tried so hard for us."
- You never loved me
- I was always the outsider
- I need to stay in my lane

She casts herself as the wounded soul, and you—the logical, clear-thinking partner—suddenly feel like the heartless one.

2. SUDDEN RAGE OR MELTDOWNS

Rage is another diversion tactic. If crying does not work, she might escalate into fury:

- Slamming doors
- Screaming

- Accusations of betrayal
- Threats to leave
- Sleeping all day.
- Goes to bed when your up/ gets up from bed when you go to sleep.
- Call police blaming you.

This intensity derails the conversation. You are no longer talking about her broken promises—you're managing a crisis.

---

3. Playing the Helpless Victim

Sometimes, drama takes the form of fragility: "I can't take this anymore," or "You're pushing me too hard." She collapses emotionally to guilt you into silence.

She may bring up her mental health, past traumas, or talk about how "everyone leaves" her. It sounds vulnerable, but it's really a warning: Back off, or else.

4. Public Performances

When others are around, the theatrics often intensify. She cries louder, acts more fragile, and frames you as cold, angry, or emotionally abusive. Keeping her from bank accounts even though she does not work, just spends the money.

To outsiders, she appears as the heartbroken heroine. Meanwhile, your frustration and attempts to explain the truth come across as harsh or insensitive—because the optics have been manipulated.

Dr. Paul's Story: The Day My Truth Was Drowned Out by Her lies

I once confronted her gently about how she belittled me in front of others. Before I could finish a sentence, she burst into rage —loud, dramatic, visible to everyone nearby.

Suddenly I wasn't a man expressing hurt—I was the monster who "crushed her spirit." People rushed to comfort her. I stood there, humiliated, unheard, and furious—not just at her, but at myself for letting it happen again.

That was the day I stopped trying to win with logic and started reclaiming my reality.

Why This Tactic Works So Well

Drama hijacks the conversation. It triggers your compassion, your protective instincts, and your discomfort with conflict. It makes you forget what the original issue was.

You stop seeking truth and start seeking peace.

But peace built on suppression is not peace at all. It's compliance. And over time, it conditions you to:

- Silence your needs
- Dismiss your feelings
- Avoid confrontation
- Walk on eggshells

This is how she trains you to stay small—so her world can stay centered on her.

Dr. Paul's Diagnostic Tool: The Accountability Flip Test

When you raise an issue, ask yourself:

> Does this conversation quickly flip back to me being the problem?
>
> Am I left apologizing, defending, or emotionally managing her—instead of addressing the original issue?

If so, you're not being heard. You're being handled.

How to Resist Emotional Hijacking

1. **Don't Match Her Intensity**

Stay calm. Don't argue with the performance. Say, "I'm here to talk about the issue, not react to emotional outbursts."If you can't do that then forget it.

1. **Anchor the Topic**

Keep repeating the core point:
"We're not discussing your reaction—we're discussing what happened."
"Let's come back to the behavior, not just the feelings about it."

1. **Use Reflective Boundaries**

"If you need time to calm down, I'll step away. But we're not resolving this through yelling or tears."

1. **Document Patterns**

Keep track of conversations and how they derail. It will give you clarity and validation later when your memory is under attack.

1. **Seek Outside Witnesses (Cautiously)**

In cases where manipulation is extreme, couples counseling or mediated conversations can expose patterns—if the professional is trauma-informed.

DR. PAUL'S TRUTH: HER Pain Doesn't Cancel Your Reality

She may cry. She may rage. She may melt into a puddle of helplessness. But that doesn't erase what she did. Her emotions are real—but they're not always relevant to the truth you're trying to express.

You are allowed to hold her accountable. You are allowed to speak the truth. And you are allowed to walk away when theatrics replace honesty.

Chapter 10: Financial Strings and Mental Chains — How She Keeps You Hooked Without a Rope

You don't need bars to be in prison.

Sometimes, all it takes is fear—of financial ruin, emotional collapse, social isolation, or losing contact with your children. The female narcissist knows this. And that's why, even without yelling, hitting, or threats, she can hold you hostage.

She controls you with what I call financial strings and mental chains—subtle, calculated dependencies that keep you stuck, long after the love has faded.

As, I've helped untangle these invisible shackles. I've also lived them. Whether through shared bank accounts, threats about divorce, or mental conditioning that makes you doubt your survival without her—this trap is as real as any age. And it's time to break free. And that is what I did January 5th,2024. Due to her Protection Order she file in Tennessee on Dec 18th, 2023, with no communication to resolve this we were done. (December 17th around 8:30 pm after 19 facetime calls she answered the phone looking disheveled and hurried with the house completely dark and would not answer any of my questions nor explain why she could not answer the phone. I got angry and got loud . It apparently gave her the fuel she needed to. Carry out the PO. That began to cost me 10s of thousands. To defend myself and it goes on till this date in 2025.

The Illusion of Partnership

At first, the relationship may feel like a team effort. Finances are combined. Decisions are mutual. You trust her with access to your world.

But as the dynamic shifts, so does the balance of power:

- She watches your spending but hides hers.
- She "borrows" but never repays.
- She uses money as a bargaining chip for affection or peace.
- She makes you feel guilty for wanting autonomy—financial or otherwise.

Before long, what began as cooperation becomes control.

Financial Control Tactics Used by Female Narcissists

1. Financial Dependency Creation

She may quit her job, or get fired avoid contributing, or overspend recklessly forcing you to carry the burden.

At first, it may feel like support. Later, it becomes weaponized:

- "Without me, you'd have no family."
- "You'd be heartless to leave me—I gave up everything for you."
- I loss my house because of you
- Lost my Car because of you

But the truth? You're not being loved—you're being leveraged.

2. SABOTAGING YOUR Stability

Some narcissists undermine your career or reputation:

- Starting fights before work
- Making you look unstable to colleagues or family
- Creating chaos that distracts you from your goals

- Make statements in front of friends that are just off blaming you.

She wants you stretched thin, because a strong, financially secure man is harder to control.

3. Threats of Financial Destruction

If you talk about leaving, she warns:

- "I'll take everything in the divorce."
- "You'll be broke without me."
- "You'll never see me again."

These are not fears—they're weapons. And they work, because financial ruin is a powerful deterrent. And its happened to me.

4. Withholding or Misusing Shared Resources

She may:

- Refuse to pay shared bills
- Max out joint credit cards
- Hide money in private accounts
- Block access to financial records
- Stash money she retrieved from "cash back" at different stores

Suddenly, the man who once paid all the bills is mindful of bank accounts with out her on them.

Psychological Chains: The Beliefs That Bind You

Even more insidious than financial abuse is mental bondage. The female narcissist programs you to believe:

- You can't survive without her.
- You'll destroy your life by leaving.
- No other woman will love you or want you.
- You're lucky I put up with you.
- You'll be all alone.

These aren't facts. They're psychological toxins, injected slowly over time until you stop seeing any path forward except the one that leads through her approval.

Dr. Paul's Reality Check: You Are Not Powerless

I remember looking at my bank account and realizing I had no idea where the money had gone. She handled it all—until she used it to control me. I was working, earning, giving—but never really free.

And yet, the moment I decided that my dignity was worth more than my comfort, I began to rebuild.

I found that control was only effective as long as I agreed to stay small.

How to Break Financial and Mental Control

1. Start Quietly Separating Finances

If it's safe to do so:

- Open a private checking account
- Save small amounts of cash regularly
- Stop sharing passwords or account access
- Review your credit report for unknown activity

You don't need to announce your independence—you need to build it.

2. Create an Escape Budget

Begin planning:

- Legal fees
- Housing
- Transportation
- Emergency funds

The less she controls your logistics, the less she controls you.

---

3. Replace "I Can't" With "How Can I?"

Don't say, "I can't leave." Ask, "How can I prepare to leave?" Shift from fear to strategy. You'll be surprised what opens up when you reframe the question.

---

4. Reprogram Your Mindset

Use statements like:

- "I have value, even if she denies it."
- "I am not dependent—I've been conditioned."
- "Freedom may cost something, but staying is costing me everything."

5. Seek Legal and Financial Allies

- Talk to an attorney—even before leaving
- Consult a financial advisor privately
- Join support groups for men in high-conflict divorces or narcissistic abuse

You are not the first man to face this. But you can be the first in your life to break the cycle.

Dr. Paul's Final Truth: She May Own the Keys, But You Still Own Your Life

She may control you. She may control the narrative. She may even control the household.

But she doesn't control your courage.

You have the power to reclaim your freedom—financially, emotionally, spiritually. The path may not be easy, but it is real. And it starts with one firm belief:

You are not hers to manage. You are yours to rebuild.

Chapter 11: The Smear Campaign — When She Destroys Your Name to Save Her Image

You don't have to leave her to lose your reputation. Sometimes, all it takes is standing up for yourself. She would send videos /recording to any friend she had of our arguments without me knowing.

The female narcissist does not just seek control over you—she wants control over how others see you. And when she feels that control slipping, she launches a smear campaign: a targeted, deceptive, and emotionally charged assault on your character, designed to isolate you and protect her false identity.

And in this chapter, I will guide you through what to expect when she turns others against you—and how to preserve your dignity and truth even as she tries to burn your name to the ground.

What is a Smear Campaign?

A smear campaign is the narcissist's PR war. She spreads misinformation to:

- Gain sympathy
- Reinforce her victim narrative
- Destroy your credibility
- Preemptively discredit your truth
- Clam abuse

She'll paint you as the abuser, the addict, the narcissist, the unstable one—even while she's the one engaging in emotional warfare behind closed doors. And drinks and smokes. Yes , Im a good old red-neck from the south, and I drink beer , as did all my friends it was a part of our southern connection, and yes I started smoking when into 5 years of marriage until June 19th 2025 I STOPPED COLD!

Why It Happens

Narcissists are image-obsessed. They fear exposure more than anything else. So when they sense:

- You're pulling away
- You're seeking support
- You're preparing to leave
- You're beginning to speak the truth

They act swiftly to destroy your reputation before you can share your side. This is exactly what she did. In mass media.

Common Smear Campaign Tactics

1. Victimhood Varnish

She paints herself as the long-suffering partner:

- "He's so emotionally distant."
- "I've tried everything to save our relationship."
- "He's changed—he's not the man I married."
- Im depressed all the time

All vague enough to be believed, but powerful enough to frame you as the villain.

2. Character Assassination

She plants toxic seeds with anyone who will listen:

- "He's angry all the time."
- "He has control issues."
- "I think he might be dangerous."
- He is mentally abusive".
- He has the little man syndrome.
- Your not even 6' tall only real men are 6'tall.

Even if untrue, these words stain your name. Especially if you're calm and respectful—because she'll say you're just "hiding your true nature."

3. Social Sabotage

She recruits mutual friends, family, or even your children into her narrative. You may suddenly find:

- Friends ghosting you
- Family doubting you
- Colleagues avoiding you
- Poisoned jeer family for more allies

It feels like the walls are closing in. That is the point.

4. Preemptive Defense

If she senses you might speak out, she strikes first:

- "He's probably going to say some crazy things—I'm just warning you."
- "He's trying to make me look bad because he can't handle the truth."

She poisons the well so that if (and when) you speak your truth, people question your motives.

5. ONLINE ATTACKS

Some narcissists take it digital—posting vague accusations, private screenshots, or carefully curated stories to social media to win the crowd. Or even post our private argument I did not know she recorded online.

The court of public opinion becomes her playground, and your silence is seen as guilt.

Dr. Paul's Personal Battle: Watching My Character Get Rewritten

I remember hearing what she was saying about me—things that made me question whether people I'd known for decades would believe her version of me. She didn't need to scream or lie outright. All she had to do was imply that I was "emotionally abusive" or "not well."

And the most painful part? Some people believed her. Because she cried louder. Because she spoke first. Because they did not know what covert abuse looked like.

But over time, those who know my heart may come back. And those who did not—I let them go. With grace, but without apology. (Never contact me again)

Why the Smear Campaign Hurts So Deeply

Because it's not just about what she says—it's about what it costs you:

- Your sense of justice
- Your social safety net
- Your professional image
- Your emotional security

You feel stripped of your ability to explain, defend, or even exist without suspicion. That's exactly what she wants: for you to feel isolated and defeated before the real separation even begins.

How to Survive—and Win—Against the Smear

1. Don't React Emotionally

It is tempting to defend yourself, argue, or expose her lies in public. Do not. That is what she wants—proof that you are "unhinged." Instead, respond calmly, or not at all. You see I fell into that trap she would post on TikTok, and others lies about me, I would look and respond on my TikTok, I know, childish.... Love or the thought of love does make you a little nut ....

2. Protect Your Reputation Strategically

- Keep records: texts, emails, voice messages.
- Document false accusations.
- Maintain consistent, respectful communication with mutual contacts.
- Share your story privately with trusted allies—not everyone needs the truth, just the right people.

3. Stay on the High Road—But Don't Be Silent

You don't have to match her drama, but you don't have to stay invisible, either. A well-timed truth spoken in calm, credible language is more powerful than a dozen lies shouted in pain.

Use phrases like:

- "I respect your opinion, but there's more to the story than she's shared."
- "My goal isn't to bash anyone, but I won't allow lies to go unchecked."
- "Those who know me, know my character."

4. Focus on Your Circle, Not the Crowd

You do not need to "clear your name" with everyone. Focus on those who matter: your children, your close friends, your professional contacts. Let them see your integrity.

5. Prepare for Legal Battles Wisely

If false accusations escalate to custody disputes or legal claims, get documentation early. Truth matters in court—but only when it's recorded, organized, and calmly presented.

Dr. Paul's Final Truth: Your Reputation is Rebuildable—Your Dignity is Not Disposable

She may have tarnished your name in some circles. But your character remains untouched. And the people who truly matter—the ones with wisdom and discernment—will eventually see through her show.

Never forget: lies are loud. Truth is patient.

Chapter 12: Rebuilding the Man Within — The First Steps Toward Healing and Wholeness

You survived the confusion, the manipulation, the betrayal. You made it out—or you're preparing to. That alone is proof of your strength.

But what now?

What happens when the silence sets in, the adrenaline fades, and you realize you're not just out of a toxic relationship—you're standing in the wreckage of a life that no longer feels like your own?

I am here to tell as this chapter marks the beginning of a new chapter in your life. One that is no longer defined by her moods, her lies, or her power. One that is rooted in rebuilding your identity, reestablishing your worth, and recovering your peace.

Why Healing Feels So Foreign

After narcissistic abuse, especially from a female partner, healing can feel confusing—because the damage wasn't always visible. There were no broken bones, no screaming fights every night. Just a slow erosion of self:

- You question your instincts.
- You doubt your memory.
- You feel guilty for leaving—or for staying so long.
- You miss the person she pretended to be.
- You struggle to trust anyone—including yourself.

This is all normal. You are not weak. You are wounded. And wounds can heal—if they're acknowledged and cared for.

STEP 1: RECLAIM YOUR Reality

Gaslighting, shame, and emotional sabotage make you question what was real. So the first step is owning the truth of what happened to you:

> She manipulated you.
>
> She exploited your empathy.
>
> She hurt you, intentionally.
>
> And you are not to blame for her behavior.

Write it down. Speak it aloud. Call it what it was. Your healing begins when the fog lifts and the truth stands.

Step 2: Grieve the Illusion

One of the hardest parts of recovering from a narcissistic relationship is grieving not just the person—but the promise.

You may miss:

- The woman she pretended to be.
- The future you planned.
- The version of yourself you once were with her.

Let yourself grieve. Cry if needed. Journal. Talk. Mourn the illusion—so you can make space for something real.

Step 3: Rebuild Routine and Structure

Narcissistic chaos disrupts your life rhythm. To regain control, create order:

- Wake up at the same time each day.
- Eat nourishing food.
- Move your body—walk, lift, stretch.
- Go to bed at a consistent hour.

These small disciplines are not trivial. They remind your nervous system: I am safe now. I am in charge now.

STEP 4: RECONNECT WITH Self-Trust

Abuse made you second-guess everything. Healing means learning to trust your inner voice again:

- Practice small, independent decisions daily.
- Keep promises to yourself—no matter how minor.
- Journal thoughts and revisit them later to see how often your gut was right.
- Celebrate every time you stand in your truth, even if it's uncomfortable.

Step 5: Choose Who You Let In

After betrayal, you may fear relationships altogether. That is understandable. But isolation breeds more pain.

Choose carefully, not fearfully. Seek people who:

- Listen without judging.
- Validate without rescuing.
- Respect your space.
- Don't minimize what you went through.

These people exist. Start with one. Then two. Let your circle grow at your speed.

Dr. Paul's Personal Practice: The Mirror Exercise

For weeks after my separation, I stood in front of the mirror every morning and said:

> "I'm not who she said I was.
>
> I am strong.
>
> I am sane.
>
> I am worthy of real love."

At first it felt forced. But over time, I believed it again. And eventually, I lived it.

You can too.

Step 6: Engage in Purposeful Healing

Healing does not happen automatically. It requires active participation. Consider:

- Therapy — especially with someone trained in narcissistic abuse
- Support groups for male survivors
- Books, podcasts, courses — curated content from voices that understand
- Coaching for rebuilding identity and direction

Don't wait until you're "completely broken" to seek help. Start now. Healing isn't weakness—it's power.

Step 7: Redefine Masculinity and Strength

The female narcissist often attacks a man's masculinity—calling him weak, short, or other ways to demean you, for having emotions, unstable for speaking up, needy for having needs.

Reject that lie.

True masculinity is not about stoicism—it's about integrity, courage, and self-respect.

You are not weak for crying.

You are not soft for walking away.

You are not broken—you are becoming.

Dr. Paul's Final Insight: Who You Were Is Not Lost—He's Just Been Buried

Beneath the shame, the fear, the conditioning... is still you.

The man who loved deeply.

The man who stood with honor.

The man who believed in commitment and truth.

That man is not gone—he's just been overwritten by survival mode.

Now, it's time to reintroduce yourself... to yourself.

Chapter 13: The Boundary Rebuild — Learning to Say No and Mean It

If narcissistic abuse had a blueprint, one of its foundational cracks would be this: **the erosion of boundaries.**

She didn't just ignore your "no." She rewrote it. Mocked it. Punished it. She taught you—consciously or subconsciously—that your needs were selfish, your limits were rude, and your discomfort was less important than her desires.

But here's the truth: boundaries are not walls. They are doors with locks—you decide who enters, how long they stay, and how they behave while they are in your life.

As I have worked on setting boundaries would make them "difficult," "cold," or "toxic." But the reality is the opposite: clear boundaries are the beginning of self-respect and emotional peace.

What Are Boundaries, Really?

Boundaries are not about controlling others. They're about defining your limits and protecting your energy.

They communicate:

- What you will and won't tolerate
- How you expect to be spoken to
- What kind of behavior earns access to you
- What consequences follow when someone violates your limits

Healthy boundaries are assertive, not aggressive. Firm, not inflexible. Loving, not enabling.

Why Narcissists Hate Boundaries

Because boundaries do what the narcissist fears most: limit their control.

When you set a boundary, you say:

- "You don't own my emotions."
- "You can't define my worth."
- "I won't tolerate disrespect, even if you call it love."

To a female narcissist, this is treason. That's why she punished your boundaries through:

- Guilt-tripping: "I guess I'm just not good enough for you now."
- Rage: "You've changed. You're heartless."
- Ridicule: "Oh, look who's finally growing a backbone."
- Reversal: "You're the controlling one!"

She twisted your healthy growth into a character flaw—so you'd shrink again. But not anymore.

Signs Your Boundaries Were Broken

Ask yourself:

Did I feel afraid to say "no"?

Did I over-explain myself constantly?

Did I allow behavior that made me uncomfortable just to keep the peace?

Did I feel guilt after expressing my needs?

Did I tolerate repeated disrespect?

If the answer is yes, you weren't being weak—you were being manipulated. But you can reclaim your power. Starting now.

The Five Essential Boundary Zones

1. **Emotional Boundaries**

Example: "I won't be yelled at, insulted, or emotionally dumped on."

1. **Time Boundaries**

Example: "I'm not available 24/7 to solve your problems."

1. **Communication Boundaries**

Example: "If you talk over me or twist my words, I'll end the conversation."

1. **Physical Boundaries**

Example: "I choose who touches me, when, and how."

1. **Digital Boundaries**

Example: "I don't share passwords, and I don't tolerate monitoring of my private conversations."

Dr. Paul's Core Rule: Boundaries Without Consequences Are Just Suggestions

If someone breaks your boundary and nothing happens—they learn your limits are negotiable.

That's why every boundary must come with a consequence you're willing to enforce:

- "If you raise your voice, I'll leave the room."
- "If you insult me, I'll hang up the phone."
- "If you lie again, I will walk away from this relationship."

You don't need to shout. You don't need to convince. You just need to follow through.

How to Rebuild Your Boundary Muscles

1. Start Small

Don't try to set 10 boundaries at once. Begin with one:

> "I won't respond to texts after 9 PM."
>
> "I need 24 hours to think before making major decisions."

Practice holding the line. The confidence will grow.

---

2. Drop the Guilt

You are not selfish for saying "no." You are sovereign. And if someone makes you feel guilty for honoring your limits, that says more about them than you.

---

3. Use Direct, Clear Language

Weak boundary:

"I just really don't like when you kind of do that."

Strong boundary:

"Don't raise your voice at me. If you do, I'll step away from the conversation."

---

4. Prepare for Pushback

People who benefited from your lack of boundaries will resist the new you. Let them. Stand tall. You are not responsible for their discomfort with your growth.

5. Affirm Your Right to Peace

Say it to yourself every morning:

"I don't need permission to protect my peace."

"My needs are valid."

"Boundaries are a form of love—for me and for others."

DR. PAUL'S PERSONAL Boundary Revelation

The day I first enforced a boundary—not with anger, but with calm conviction—I felt fear, then guilt, then... freedom.

And I knew: This is what it means to reclaim your manhood—not through dominance, but through self-possession.

Final Truth: Boundaries Are Not Barriers—They Are Bridges to Peace

You're not pushing people away by setting boundaries. You're inviting only those who can respect and reciprocate.

If someone leaves your life because of your boundary, they were never there to honor you—only to exploit you.

Let them go. And build something better.

Chapter 14: Trust After Trauma — Learning to Love Again, Starting With Yourself

Of all the damage narcissistic abuse leaves behind, broken trust may be the most haunting. Not just trust in others, but trust in yourself—your judgment, your instincts, your capacity to love wisely.

You begin to ask:

- How did I not see it sooner?
- How can I ever trust another woman again?
- How can I trust myself to make better choices next time?

These questions aren't signs of weakness. They're the first indicators that you're healing—because they mean you're searching for truth, not fantasy.

As, I've sat with men who blamed themselves, shut down emotionally, or vowed never to love again. But here's what I tell them—and now I tell you:

> Trust is not dead. It's just buried under betrayal. And it can be resurrected.

Understanding the Trust Breakdown

Let's be clear: she trained you to mistrust yourself.

Through:

- Gaslighting
- False accusations
- Emotional bait-and-switch
- Projection of her sins onto you

She shattered your internal compass and left you spinning. That's not your fault—it was her strategy.

And like any strategy, it loses power once you see it clearly.

Why Trust Feels Dangerous After Narcissistic Abuse

Trust requires openness. But after trauma, openness feels like vulnerability—and vulnerability feels like danger.

So you shut down. You isolate. You build emotional walls around yourself and call them "boundaries." But here's the truth:

> Healthy love doesn't require you to let your guard down all at once—just to let it down intentionally.

THE THREE TRUSTS YOU Must Rebuild

---

1. Trust in Your Own Perception

The narcissist distorted your reality until you couldn't tell truth from manipulation. It's time to reclaim your gut.

How?

- Start journaling what you see, hear, and feel in real-time
- Compare how often your first instinct turns out to be right

- Talk to a therapist or coach to recalibrate your internal radar

Repetition is key. Repetition creates confidence. And confidence rebuilds trust.

---

2. Trust in Your Emotions

Narcissists often label your emotional responses as "overreactions." Over time, you suppress your feelings just to keep the peace.

But your emotions are not flaws. They are information.

- Anger? It means a boundary was crossed.
- Sadness? It means something mattered.
- Anxiety? It means something feels unsafe.
- Joy? It means you're reconnecting with yourself.

Instead of shaming your feelings, listen to them.

3. Trust in Healthy People Again

This may be the hardest part—especially if your narcissist used others in her abuse campaign. But isolation is its own kind of prison.

You can trust again. Just not blindly.

Watch for these green flags:

- People who listen more than they speak
- People who own their mistakes without blaming
- People who respect your pace
- People who don't need to be the center of every interaction
- People who consistently align words with actions

Rebuilding trust isn't about finding perfect people. It's about surrounding yourself with people who are safe, not perfect.

Dr. Paul's Reflection: I Had to Trust Myself First

I spent months after my relationship doubting my ability to see red flags. But slowly, I realized—I did see them. I just explained them away. I minimized them to maintain the illusion.

So I made a vow:

> "Next time I feel something is wrong, I won't ignore it. I'll pause, I'll ask, and I'll act—without shame."

That one decision restored more of my inner authority than any book, any therapy session, or any apology ever could.

You can make that vow, too.

How to Begin Rebuilding Trust Today

Create a "Truth Timeline"

Write out the events of the relationship. Label what you knew, what you felt, what you ignored. See how your body and mind were telling you the truth—even when you doubted yourself.

Practice Micro-Trust Decisions

- Choose a restaurant.
- Make a new friend.
- Say no when you mean it.
- Say yes when you want to.

Each act of self-trust is a brick in the foundation of your new life.

Set Relationship Standards, Not Fears

Don't build your future around avoiding narcissists. Build it around attracting honesty, humility, and reciprocity.

Your standards should sound like:

> "I only invest in people who show emotional consistency."

"If someone avoids accountability, I remove access."

"My peace is more important than anyone's potential."

ACKNOWLEDGE THE RISK—THEN Take It Anyway

Yes, you may get hurt again. But pain caused by trying is far more honorable than the slow death of emotional isolation.

You don't heal from betrayal by staying guarded forever. You heal by becoming a man who chooses wisely, listens deeply, and walks away quickly when red flags wave.

DR. PAUL'S FINAL TRUTH: You Were Not Stupid—You Were Sincere

You loved with an open heart. You believed the best in someone. That is not a flaw. That is human courage.

And it means this: your capacity to love is still intact. It just needs to be redirected—first toward yourself, then toward someone who truly deserves it.

Chapter 15: Freedom Maintenance — How to Avoid Getting Hooked Again

Escaping a narcissist is a triumph. But staying free? That is mastery.

Narcissists come in many forms—charming, wounded, spiritual, successful, seductive. Once you've been through the emotional war zone of one, it is easy to assume you will spot the next a mile away.

But here is the truth:

> They rarely look the same. But they always feel the same.

The Narcissist Playbook (In Disguise)

By now, you know the obvious red flags. But female narcissists in particular often repackage the same toxic traits in softer, more socially acceptable wrapping:

- The "wounded empath" who seems deeply spiritual—but never takes accountability
- The "strong, independent woman" who subtly needs you to validate her every move
- The "ride or die" partner who becomes controlling in the name of love
- The "free spirit" who avoids responsibility, blames exes, and expects you to fix her

What these women have in common isn't their image—it's their impact.

THEY MAKE YOU FEEL:

- Confused
- Over-responsible
- Emotionally imbalanced
- Like you owe them something just for being loved

Pay attention to how you feel, not just how they present.

The Real Reason You Might Be Vulnerable Again

After narcissistic abuse, your nervous system is used to chaos. Emotional highs and lows can feel familiar—even addictive.

You might mistake:

- Intensity for intimacy
- Possessiveness for passion
- Love bombing for chemistry
- Fixing someone for bonding

That's why relapse prevention starts with reconditioning yourself to seek peace over performance.

Dr. Paul's Five Golden Rules of Narcissist Prevention

1. Take Your Time

Narcissists move fast. They want to lock you in before you see the truth. Slow down your dating. Delay commitment. Give space for real patterns to emerge.

Remember:

> If it feels like a whirlwind, step out of the storm.

---

2. Believe Patterns, Not Apologies

One-time mistakes can be forgiven. Repeated ones are patterns. If she:

- Blames others constantly
- Can't tolerate feedback
- Overreacts to small things
- Charms everyone except you behind closed doors
- Makes you feel guilty for asserting needs

...you don't need proof she's a narcissist. You just need to leave.

3. Don't Ignore Gut Checks

If something feels off, it usually is. Don't override your instincts because you "don't want to judge."

A red flag doesn't need a second opinion. Your discomfort is enough.

---

4. KEEP YOUR IDENTITY Independent

The healthiest relationships come when both people maintain:

- Friendships
- Passions
- Financial autonomy
- Emotional regulation
- Private time

If she needs to merge completely to feel secure, you're not building love—you're building entrapment.

---

5. Watch How She Handles the Word "No"

Set a boundary early on. See how she responds. A healthy woman will respect it—even if she disagrees. A narcissist will:

- Guilt trip
- Flirt harder
- Freeze you out
- Make it about your "fear of intimacy"

This simple test can save you years of pain.

Dr. Paul's Practice: The "One-Month Mirror"

After meeting someone new, pause at the one-month mark. Ask yourself:

- Have I already compromised any values?
- Am I spending energy explaining or defending myself?
- Do I feel more grounded—or more anxious?
- Have I been love-bombed, trauma-dumped, or isolated from friends?

If the answer triggers alarm, exit now. Early pain is cheaper than long-term collapse.

How to Stay Grounded Between Relationships

1. Stay focused on your healing—not your next partner

Love yourself first. Not as a cliché—but as a conscious, daily act.

1. Create a "non-negotiables" list
    - Emotional maturity
    - Respectful disagreement
    - Personal accountability
    - Honesty over charm

Post it where you'll see it.

1. Talk to your future self

Ask: What would healed me choose right now?
What would hurt me settle for?

Let the healed you lead. Not the lonely you.

FINAL TRUTH FROM DR. Paul: Your Freedom Wasn't Given—It Was Earned

You've fought to escape the grasp of someone who wanted to shape your reality, crush your confidence, and feed on your compassion. That was war.

This is reconstruction.

Protect your peace like it's oxygen—because it is. Don't chase another person to finish your healing. Finish your healing so no one can ever take it from you again.

•

Chapter 16: Life Beyond the Storm — Creating a Future That's Yours Alone

You've walked through the fire. You've untangled the lies. You've buried the version of yourself that once begged for scraps of love.

And now?

It's time to rebuild—not a version of life you once had, but a future that's been fully claimed by you.

This chapter isn't about narcissists. It's about you. Your strength. Your goals. Your joy. Your future.

I am Dr. Paul J. Peloquin Sr., PhD, and I wrote this chapter for the man who refuses to live defined by pain. The man who knows he is not just a survivor—but a creator of the next chapter of his life.

WHAT "LIFE AFTER" REALLY Looks Like

It's not a straight line. There are days when you'll still hear her voice in your head. Days when you wonder if healing means being alone. Days when you feel exhausted by the emotional work.

But if you stay the course, you'll notice changes:

- You laugh more easily.
- You sleep deeper.
- You no longer flinch when your phone dings.
- You walk into rooms with your chest higher.
- You attract people who see you, not just use you.

That is what life beyond the storm looks like: not perfect, but peaceful.

From Recovery to Rediscovery

Narcissistic abuse doesn't just hurt—it robs you of identity.

You may have lost:

- Your voice
- Your hobbies
- Your vision
- Your confidence
- Your sense of purpose

Now it's time to take it back.

Step 1: Redefine Who You Are—Without Her Narrative

She told you who you were:

- Too sensitive
- Too selfish
- Too controlling
- Too emotional

Now it's time to ask: Who do I say I am?

Take inventory of your truth:

- What do I value?
- What kind of man do I want to be?
- What do I want to be known for?

Write your identity in your own words. Reclaim authorship of your story.

Step 2: Reignite Your Passions

What did you give up to keep the peace? What activities, friendships, or interests fell away because they "bothered" her?

Make a list of everything you used to love. Then slowly begin to reintroduce one at a time. Even five minutes a day matters.

You don't need permission to enjoy your life anymore.

Step 3: Create a Future Goal Map

Abuse keeps you stuck in survival mode. Healing propels you toward legacy.

Map out:

- Short-term goals (3–6 months)
- Medium-term goals (1–2 years)
- Long-term goals (5–10 years)

These can include:

- Travel
- Business ventures
- Creative projects
- Healthy relationships
- Giving back to others

Set timelines. Revisit them monthly. Let progress replace pain.

Dr. Paul's Personal Reset: From Recovery to Purpose

There was a time when I woke up dreading the day. No passion, no vision—just emotional exhaustion.

But once I chose to live with purpose for myself, not in reaction to what I'd survived, everything changed.

I didn't just get better. I got clear. And from that clarity came confidence.

You have that power too.

Daily Habits for Post-Narcissist Thriving

Morning Mindset Reset

Start the day with these affirmations:

- "I am safe now."
- "I am enough."
- "I choose peace over performance."
- "I honor myself today."

Physical Movement

Healing isn't just mental—it's physiological. Move your body daily to discharge stored trauma and restore vitality. Walk, stretch, lift, breathe.

Emotional Hygiene

You brush your teeth—now brush your emotions:

- Journal
- Reflect
- Speak honestly
- Cry when needed
- Laugh often

Your feelings are data—not dysfunction.

INTENTIONAL SOCIAL Circles

Surround yourself with people who:

- Value your truth
- Don't need to be impressed
- Respect your boundaries
- Add to your peace, not just your calendar

Weekly Purpose Check-In

Every week, ask:

- What am I building?
- What drained me this week?
- What brought me joy?
- Who am I becoming?

This keeps your post-abuse life from becoming passive.

The Freedom of No Longer Needing to Prove Anything

When you were with her, you probably lived in performance mode: trying to prove your worth, fix the relationship, justify your decisions.

But now?

> You don't need to prove anything. Just live fully.
>
> Be honest. Be kind. Be bold. Be still. Be exactly who you are—without apology or edit.

That's real freedom.

Dr. Paul's Final Truth: You Didn't Just Survive Her—You Outgrew Her

She didn't break you. She revealed where your healing needed to happen.

Now that you've done the work, now that you've chosen growth over bitterness, you have become the man she could never manipulate again.

And better yet—you've become the man the world needs.

A man who:

- Sets boundaries without guilt
- Walks in truth without fear
- Loves without losing himself
- Leads with honor, not ego

That's you now. That's life beyond the storm.

Chapter 17: From Wounded to Witness — How to Help Other Men Find the Exit

There comes a moment in every survivor's journey when healing turns outward. You've done the work. You've found your footing. And now, a question arises from deep inside:

> What if I could help someone else escape what I went through?

Not from ego. Not for validation. But because you remember what it felt like to suffer in silence. You remember the confusion, the shame, the nights spent wondering if it was your fault.

This chapter is about stepping into your next role—not as a victim, not just as a survivor, but as a witness. A mentor. A guidepost for other men who are still lost in the fog.

Why Your Voice Matters

Male victims of narcissistic abuse are often invisible. Silenced by stigma. Dismissed by courts. Mocked by society. Even therapists miss the signs—because they don't expect a woman to be the abuser.

That's why your voice matters.

Because when another man hears your story, he doesn't just gain information—he gains permission. Permission to admit what's happening. Permission to feel. Permission to leave.

You don't have to have a degree to speak the truth. You just need to tell it—clearly, boldly, and without shame.

How to Tell Your Story Safely and Powerfully

START WITH THE WHY

Don't tell your story to vent. Tell it to validate. Your purpose is to help someone else recognize the signs—and believe they're not alone.

> "I'm sharing this because I didn't know what was happening until it was almost too late. Maybe you're there right now. And maybe this will help."

Speak from the Scar, Not the Wound

Don't share when you're still triggered, raw, or reactive. Wait until you've processed enough to speak calmly—even if your voice shakes. Trauma shared too early can retraumatize both you and your audience.

Be Specific, Not Graphic

You don't need to recount every insult or betrayal. Focus on the patterns:

- Emotional gaslighting
- Shame cycles
- Isolation tactics
- Control dynamics

Let the listener connect the dots without drowning them in your darkest moments.

CENTER YOUR GROWTH

End every story with what you've learned, how you're healing, and what you'd say to your former self.

That's where your credibility comes from—not just your pain, but your progress.

Where and How to Help Other Men

You don't have to start a podcast or write a book (though you can). Start with one of these:

1. Private Conversations

You probably already know a man who's struggling. He may not say it, but he needs an opening.

Try:

> "You ever feel like you can't be yourself in your relationship?"
>
> "I've been through something rough—I'd share it with you if you ever want to talk."

That's enough to crack the door.

2. ONLINE COMMUNITIES

Join forums, support groups, or platforms for male survivors. Contribute your story. Offer feedback. Celebrate wins. Be the voice of nonjudgmental clarity.

---

3. Write, Record, or Teach

- Blog about your journey
- Speak on panels or in men's groups
- Start a support circle at a church or community center
- Share content anonymously if you prefer

Use whatever platform feels natural. What matters is that your experience reaches someone.

---

4. Advocate for Legal Reform in family law and Mental Health Awareness

Once healed, consider using your experience to advocate:

- For family court reform
- For better training in recognizing female narcissistic abuse
- For equitable treatment of male victims in shelters and counseling services

When enough men speak out, the system has to change.

Dr. Paul's Experience: The First Time I Told My Truth

The first time I publicly spoke about my experience, I expected skepticism. I braced for judgment.

But instead, I got messages like:

> "I thought I was the only one."
>
> "You just described my marriage."
>
> "Thank you. You helped me understand what I couldn't explain."

That's when I knew: telling your truth is an act of service.

You may never know the lives you save by sharing yours. But I promise—there will be some.

Boundaries When Helping Others

Helping doesn't mean:

- Becoming someone's therapist
- Absorbing their pain
- Saving them from their choices

You can support without sacrificing:

- Listen, but don't fix
- Encourage, but don't chase
- Speak truth, but let them act on it themselves

You are a guide, not a savior.

Final Truth from Dr. Paul: Wounds Become Wisdom When Shared

You didn't choose this experience. But you can choose what it becomes.

- A curse?
- A life sentence?
- Or a calling?

If even one man walks away from abuse because of your courage, it was worth it.

You don't have to shout. Just speak clearly. Speak truth. And keep walking as proof that freedom is possible.

Chapter 18: Redefining Love — How to Give and Receive It Without Losing Yourself Again

After surviving the manipulation, gaslighting, and trauma of a relationship with a narcissistic woman, the idea of love may feel... conflicted.

Maybe even dangerous.

You might think:

- What if I get fooled again?
- How can I ever trust another woman?
- Do I even want love anymore?

These are honest questions—and they're rooted in truth. Because what you experienced wasn't love. It was control disguised as intimacy.

Now it's time to redefine love for yourself—not as a risk, but as a reward for the man you've become.

In this chapter, we will explore how to open your heart without closing your eyes, how to love without enabling, and how to receive love that nourishes rather than depletes.

What Love Isn't

Before we define healthy love, let's name what it isn't. Love is not:

- Emotional dependency
- Being responsible for someone else's happiness
- Performing to avoid conflict
- Tolerating lies, insults, or manipulation
- "Fixing" someone in the name of compassion

You may have called these things love in the past. You may have sacrificed your dignity for the illusion of connection. But real love doesn't demand that you shrink to stay safe.

Real love is where you expand.

The Five Pillars of Healthy Love

1. Emotional Safety

You feel calm around this person—not on edge. You can speak freely, disagree respectfully, and express emotion without fear of punishment or mockery.

Love should feel safe, not suspenseful.

2. Mutual Responsibility

You don't carry the entire emotional load. She takes ownership of her own mood, past, triggers, and growth. There's no scorekeeping—just partnership.

3. Truth-Telling

In healthy love, honesty is the foundation—even when it's uncomfortable. You're not punished for being truthful. In fact, your truth is welcomed, not weaponized.

4. Freedom Within the Connection

You still have your friends, your passions, your time alone. Healthy love adds to your life—it doesn't become your entire identity.

5. Consistency Over Intensity

A narcissist loves with a boom and a crash. But real love builds slowly. It's steady, predictable, kind. It may not feel like fireworks—but it will feel like home.

Dr. Paul's Rule: If You Lose Yourself, It's Not Love

In my past relationship, I thought I was loving her. In reality, I was erasing myself to avoid rejection. I confused loyalty with submission. I called silence "peace." I called tension "passion."

It took me years to understand: if loving her requires you to betray yourself—it's not love. It's bondage.

Red Flags to Watch for in New Relationships

Even in recovery, you may still be vulnerable to charm-based manipulation. Stay alert to:

- Fast attachment: "You're the one" within days or weeks
- Over-disclosure: trauma dumps too early
- "Only you get me" language: isolation disguised as bonding
- Dismissiveness toward your boundaries
- Subtle put-downs masked as jokes

Healthy love honors your healing. It doesn't rush, twist, or pull you back into old patterns.

Green Flags: Signs You're in Healthy Territory

She respects your pace and your space

She can apologize sincerely—and change behavior

She encourages your friendships and passions

She doesn't need to win arguments—just understand you

You feel calm in her presence, not confused or constantly questioning

This is love with dignity—the kind you deserve.

How to Love Without Losing Yourself Again

Keep Your Identity Intact

- Maintain routines
- Keep your friendships
- Stay committed to your personal goals

Don't disappear into someone else's emotional world. A strong relationship is built on two whole people—not one rescuer and one project.

Keep Checking In With Yourself

Ask regularly:

"Am I still honoring my values?"

"Am I still making choices based on clarity, not fear?"

"Am I free to say no?"

If the answer is "no," reassess. Your peace is not optional.

Make Agreements, Not Assumptions

A healthy partner will want clarity:

- What does trust mean to each of you?
- What are your shared values?
- What are the deal-breakers?

Speak these aloud. Healthy love thrives on alignment, not assumption.

Lead With Love, Not Fear

Don't let past pain harden your heart. You don't need to become emotionally armored to stay safe—you need to become emotionally aware.

Say:

"I choose to love wisely, not blindly."

"I'm open—but I'm not naïve."

"I will never abandon myself to keep someone else."

DR. PAUL'S FINAL TRUTH: The Right Love Will Never Ask You to Disappear

The next chapter of your life doesn't require you to stay small. It doesn't demand silence, submission, or apology.

The right love will see you, support you, and grow beside you.

And you'll no longer settle for anything less.

Chapter 19: The Legacy of Freedom — Becoming the Man You Were Always Meant to Be

When the dust settles, when the storm has passed, when your name has been smeared and survived, and your soul has been tested and restored—what's left?

You.

Not the man she tried to shape.

Not the man who questioned his own worth.

Not the man who bent himself into silence to keep the peace.

But the man you were always meant to be: self-possessed, anchored, sovereign.

This chapter is not about survival. It's about significance. Not just avoiding narcissists—but becoming a man who lives in such truth, peace, and integrity that toxicity no longer finds a home in your life.

What Is Legacy, Really?

Legacy isn't about money. It isn't about reputation. It isn't about what people say at your funeral.

Legacy is the ripple effect of how you've lived.

- Did your children see you model strength with compassion?
- Did your friends witness your honesty, even when it cost you?
- Did the men around you learn it was okay to feel and still lead?
- Did you stop the cycle that almost destroyed you?

If so, your legacy has already begun.

The Three Marks of a Man Who Has Reclaimed His Life

1. He Lives by Principle, Not Performance

After narcissistic abuse, many men struggle with identity. We've spent years adjusting ourselves to survive her moods.

But the man who has healed doesn't ask, "What will she think?"

He asks:

> "Does this align with my values?"
>
> "Am I proud of how I handled that?"
>
> "Would I want my son to copy this behavior?"

That's integrity. And it's contagious.

2. He Leads from Within, Not Over Others

Leadership after abuse looks different. It's not about controlling people or asserting dominance.

It's about:

- Owning your voice
- Standing by your truth
- Offering stability without needing praise
- Protecting your peace like it's sacred ground

You become the kind of man others trust—not because you're loud, but because you're clear.

3. HE HEALS THE NEXT Generation

Whether you have children or not, your presence in this world affects others.

When you:

- Set boundaries
- Speak out
- Show emotion without shame
- Refuse to normalize toxic dynamics

...you're rewriting the rules for what masculinity looks like.

You are ending the cycle.

Dr. Paul's Legacy Statement: I Chose Truth Over Comfort

I could have stayed silent. I could have kept performing. I could have lived my final chapters replaying her lies.

Instead, I chose:

- To heal
- To speak
- To write
- To lead

Not because I'm special—but because I was done shrinking.

Let that be your legacy too: a man who stopped shrinking—and started standing.

How to Build Your Legacy Day by Day

Define Your Non-Negotiable's

What do you refuse to compromise ever again?

- Emotional safety?
- Mutual respect?
- Peace over chaos?

Write these. Etch them into your identity.

Mentor Someone

You don't need to be a coach or counselor. Just be available. Your pain—redeemed—becomes wisdom. And wisdom is the most masculine gift you can offer another man.

Live as You, Not in Reaction to Her

Stop defining yourself as "not her." Start defining yourself as:

- The man who honors peace
- The man who walks away when disrespected

- The man who nurtures himself as fiercely as he once nurtured someone toxic

CELEBRATE PEACE WITHOUT Guilt

You don't have to keep proving you're healed.

You're allowed to laugh. To rest. To be loved. To be happy—without apology, without waiting for the other shoe to drop.

Your peace is proof of your transformation.

Final Truth from Dr. Paul: Freedom Is a Daily Decision, Not a One-Time Escape

You escaped her—but now you must choose freedom every day:

- In your words
- In your thoughts
- In your standards
- In your relationships
- In your mindset

Freedom is not a finish line. It's a lifestyle.
You are not who she said you were.
You are not who the world misunderstood.
You are not a shadow of the man you used to be.
You are the man you were meant to become.
And that—that—is your legacy.

Chapter 20: You Are Not Alone — A Closing Letter to the Man Who Chose Himself

Dear Brother,

If you're reading this, then you've made it through something most men will never talk about—let alone survive with your soul intact.

You were blamed, shamed, gaslit, and groomed. You were made to feel small in the name of "love." You were told your instincts were wrong, your emotions were too much, your loyalty not enough.

And still—you made it here.

You chose the hard truth over the comfortable lie.

You chose healing over hiding.

You chose to face what broke you, rather than keep living fractured.

You chose yourself.

Let me say it plainly: I'm proud of you.

Not for being perfect, not for having all the answers—but for staying in the fight long enough to remember who you are.

You Are Not the Only One

There are countless men walking around with invisible bruises, unexplained anxiety, and a quiet ache in their chest that whispers, Something is wrong. Most don't have the words. Fewer have the courage. Even fewer have support.

But you?

You're now one of the few who found their way out of the fog—and into the light. And because of that, your story matters. You matter.

Whether you're 26 or 66, it's never too late to take back your life.

You are not weak for loving.

You are not soft for hoping.

You are not crazy for staying longer than you should have.

You were conditioned, not defective.

You were targeted, not foolish.

You were used, not useless.

And now, you are free.

You Are Still Capable of Love

Love didn't hurt you—manipulation did. Love didn't silence you—control did. Love didn't betray you—a narcissist disguised as love did.

So don't lock your heart away forever.

Yes, be wise. Yes, set boundaries. Yes, move slowly.

But don't give up on connection.

Because the best love is still possible—starting with the one you now give yourself.

The Mission Is Now Yours

This book may be ending, but your mission isn't.

Keep speaking up. Keep walking tall. Keep noticing red flags, and honoring green ones. Keep choosing your peace over your pride. Keep helping other men rise with you.

Every boundary you hold is a gift to the world.

Every time you say, "That's not okay," you heal something ancient.

Every time you refuse to repeat the cycle, you rewrite the future.

-Dr Paul J Peloquin Sr, PhD

A FINAL WORD FROM DR. Paul

If I could sit across from you right now, man to man, I'd say this:

I see your strength.

I see your pain.

I see your courage.

I see the fire you walked through.

And I see the light in your eyes that says you're not done yet.

You didn't just survive her—you saved yourself.

And that is the most masculine, powerful, heroic thing you will ever do.

So live the rest of your life wide open.

Whole.

Healed.

Honest.

Free.

You have earned it.

With brotherhood and belief in your future,

Dr. Paul J. Peloquin Sr., PhD

The End

About the Author

From Dr. Paul J. Peloquin Sr., PhD

This book was born out of silence.

Not the kind that comforts—but the kind that crushes. The kind that creeps into your life when you're too ashamed to speak. When you're too afraid to be disbelieved. When you've been told—over and over again—that your truth is not valid, your pain is not real, and your story is not worth telling.

I wrote Echoes of Control to prove that it is.

For years, I lived behind closed doors, enduring subtle manipulations and outright cruelty at the hands of a woman who wore a mask so well the world applauded while I quietly withered. I doubted myself. I questioned my worth. And I stayed longer than I should have—not out of weakness, but out of hope, loyalty, and the belief that love should be enough.

But some love isn't love. It's control. And some people don't want connection—they want submission.

This book is not a revenge story. It is a resurrection story.

Every chapter is a declaration: that men can be victims. That narcissistic abuse is real. That emotional trauma leaves scars just as deep as physical ones. And that no matter how long you've lived in darkness, the light is still yours to claim.

If you're reading this and you feel seen, I hope you also feel strengthened.

If you're reading this and you've survived something similar, I hope you feel validated.

And if you're still in the fog—I hope this book is your first glimpse of clarity.

You are not crazy.

You are not weak.

And you are not alone.

This is the NEW not the old normal...

– Dr. Paul J. Peloquin Sr., PhD

www.ingramcontent.com/pod-product-compliance
Lightning Source LLC
LaVergne TN
LVHW090418210926
848480LV00002B/606